# NINJA®

## Professional Blender
50-Recipe Cookbook

D1445678

Editors and Content: Meghan Reilly, Kenzie Swanhart, Elizabeth Skladany, and Daniel Davis

Recipe Development: Great Flavors Recipe Development Team

Design/Layout: Leslie Anne Feagley

Creative/Photo Director: Lauren Wiernasz

Photography: Quentin Bacon and Gary Sloan

Published in the United States of America by
Partners-In-Publishing LLC
P.O. Box 250
New Hope, PA 19838

NJ600CO ISBN: 978-1-5323-2104-7

NJ600CO_50Recipe_CBwCover_181030

10      9      8      7      6      5      4      3      2      1

Printed in China

# "CRUSHING IT"
# HAS NEVER
# BEEN EASIER.

Your ordinary blender is nice and all, but can it crush ice cubes into snow at the touch of a button? Ours can. Whether you're making smoothies for your family, soup for you, or a dinner party's worth of desserts, you need a tool with the Total Crushing® power to handle whatever you can throw at it. The good news? That power is now in your hands.

# Table of Contents

**Prep time:** 15 minutes
**Container:** 72-ounce Pitcher
**Makes:** 4 servings

# AUTUMN BALANCER

## INGREDIENTS

2 sweet potatoes, steamed, cooled

2 cups unsweetened almond milk

¼ cup maple syrup

1 teaspoon salt

1 ½ cups ice

## DIRECTIONS

1. Place all ingredients into the 72-ounce Pitcher in the order listed.

2. PULSE 3 times and blend on 3 until smooth.

DO NOT BLEND HOT INGREDIENTS.

**Prep time:** 5 minutes
**Container:** 72-ounce Pitcher
**Makes:** 4–6 servings

# AVOCADO-LADA

### INGREDIENTS

2 ripe avocados, peeled, pits removed

2 small ripe bananas

4 cups coconut water

1 ½ cups frozen pineapple chunks

### DIRECTIONS

1. Place all ingredients into the 72-ounce Pitcher in the order listed.

2. PULSE 3 times and blend on 3 until smooth.

**Prep time:** 5 minutes
**Container:** 72-ounce Pitcher
**Makes:** 3 servings

# COOL GINGER PEAR

## INGREDIENTS

3 ripe pears, cored, cut in quarters

2 cups cantaloupe chunks

1 lemon, peeled, cut in half, seeds removed

1-inch piece fresh ginger, peeled

2 cups ice

## DIRECTIONS

1. Place all ingredients into the 72-ounce Pitcher in the order listed.

2. PULSE 3 times and blend on 3 until smooth.

**Prep time:** 5 minutes
**Container:** 72-ounce Pitcher
**Makes:** 4 servings

# SOUTH OF THE BORDER

## INGREDIENTS

2 ripe avocados, peeled, pits removed

¼ cup pineapple chunks

¼ cup cilantro

¼ teaspoon cayenne pepper

2 cups water

2 cups frozen mango chunks

## DIRECTIONS

1. Place all ingredients into the 72-ounce Pitcher in the order listed.

2. PULSE 3 times and blend on 3 until smooth.

**Prep time:** 5 minutes
**Container:** 72-ounce Pitcher
**Makes:** 6 servings

# COOL HONEYDEW CUCUMBER

### INGREDIENTS

1 cucumber, peeled, cut in 1-inch chunks

2 cups honeydew melon chunks

3 cups pineapple chunks

2 cups water

2 cups ice

### DIRECTIONS

1. Place all ingredients into the 72-ounce Pitcher in the order listed.

2. PULSE 3 times and blend on 3 until smooth.

**Prep time:** 5 minutes
**Container:** 72-ounce Pitcher
**Makes:** 4 servings

# MANGO MELON MINT FUSION

## INGREDIENTS

1 cup honeydew melon chunks

1 cup mango chunks

1 cup cantaloupe chunks

4 mint leaves

1 cup water

1 ½ cups ice

## DIRECTIONS

1. Place all ingredients into the 72-ounce Pitcher in the order listed.

2. PULSE 3 times and blend on 3 until smooth.

**Prep time:** 5 minutes
**Container:** 72-ounce Pitcher
**Makes:** 4 servings

# WATERMELON LIMEADE

## INGREDIENTS

4 cups watermelon chunks

1 cup water

½ cup lime juice

¾ teaspoon light agave syrup

4 mint leaves

2 cups ice

## DIRECTIONS

1. Place all ingredients into the 72-ounce Pitcher in the order listed.

2. PULSE 3 times and blend on 3 until smooth.

**Prep time:** 5 minutes
**Container:** 72-ounce Pitcher
**Makes:** 4 servings

# ISLAND SUNRISE SMOOTHIE

## INGREDIENTS

1 cup pineapple chunks

2 cups coconut water

1 cup frozen mango chunks

1 small ripe banana

1 cup frozen strawberries

## DIRECTIONS

1. Place all ingredients into the 72-ounce Pitcher in the order listed.

2. PULSE 3 times and blend on 3 until smooth.

**Prep time:** 5 minutes
**Container:** 72-ounce Pitcher
**Makes:** 2 servings

# STRAWBERRY MELON BLAST

## INGREDIENTS

2 cups cantaloupe chunks

½ medium cucumber, peeled, cut in quarters

8 strawberries, hulled

1 cup ice

## DIRECTIONS

1. Place all ingredients into the 72-ounce Pitcher in the order listed.

2. PULSE 3 times and blend on 3 until smooth.

**Prep time:** 5 minutes
**Container:** 72-ounce Pitcher
**Makes:** 2–3 servings

# CINNAMON & COFFEE SMOOTHIE

## INGREDIENTS

½ cup strongly brewed coffee, cooled

1 square (1 ounce) dark chocolate

1 cup rice milk

1 teaspoon ground cinnamon

½ cup low-fat vanilla yogurt

4–6 ice cubes

## DIRECTIONS

1. Place all ingredients into the 72-ounce Pitcher in the order listed.

2. PULSE 3 times and blend on 3 until smooth.

DO NOT BLEND HOT INGREDIENTS.

**Prep time:** 5 minutes
**Container:** 72-ounce Pitcher
**Makes:** 4 servings

# WATERMELON QUENCH

## INGREDIENTS

2 ½ cups watermelon chunks

2 cups pomegranate juice

1 cup frozen sliced peaches

## DIRECTIONS

1. Place all ingredients into the 72-ounce Pitcher in the order listed.

2. PULSE 3 times and blend on 3 until smooth.

**Prep time:** 5 minutes
**Container:** 72-ounce Pitcher
**Makes:** 2–4 servings

# TROPICAL CHILL

## INGREDIENTS

1 ripe banana

½ cup pineapple chunks

½ cup honeydew melon chunks

½ lime, peeled, cut in half, seeds removed

¾ cup coconut water

1 cup ice

## DIRECTIONS

1. Place all ingredients into the 72-ounce Pitcher in the order listed.

2. PULSE 3 times and blend on 3 until smooth.

**Prep time:** 5 minutes
**Container:** 72-ounce Pitcher
**Makes:** 4 servings

# STRAWBERRY BANANA SMOOTHIE

## INGREDIENTS

4 small ripe bananas, cut in half

2 cups low-fat milk

¼ cup agave nectar

4 cups frozen strawberries

## DIRECTIONS

1. Place all ingredients into the 72-ounce Pitcher in the order listed.

2. PULSE 3 times and blend on 3 until smooth.

**Prep time:** 5 minutes
**Container:** 72-ounce Pitcher
**Makes:** 3 servings

# BERRY, BERRY GOOD DAY

## INGREDIENTS

½ cup raspberries

¼ cup strawberries, hulled

¼ cup blueberries

¼ cup pineapple chunks

1 tablespoon goji berries

½ cup low-fat plain yogurt

¼ cup water

6–8 ice cubes

## DIRECTIONS

1. Place all ingredients into the 72-ounce Pitcher in the order listed.

2. PULSE 3 times and blend on 3 until smooth.

# CITRUS SPIRULINA BLAST

## INGREDIENTS

2 grapefruits, peeled, cut in quarters, seeds removed

2 oranges, peeled, cut in quarters, seeds removed

2 cups pineapple chunks

¼ cup lime juice

2 teaspoons spirulina

2 cups water

2 cups ice

## DIRECTIONS

1. Place all ingredients into the 72-ounce Pitcher in the order listed.

2. PULSE 3 times and blend on 3 until smooth.

# ROASTED GARLIC & ROMA TOMATO SOUP

## INGREDIENTS

1 can (28 ounces) peeled whole tomatoes

4 cloves garlic, peeled

3 tablespoons tomato paste

¾ cup silken tofu

3 tablespoons extra virgin olive oil

½ teaspoon salt

¼ teaspoon ground black pepper

1 cup vegetable broth

1 tablespoon fresh basil leaves

## DIRECTIONS

1. Place all ingredients into the 72-ounce Pitcher in the order listed.

2. PULSE 3 times and blend on 3 until smooth.

3. Transfer soup to a large saucepan and simmer over medium-low heat for about 15 minutes, or until heated through.

DO NOT BLEND HOT INGREDIENTS.

# CREAMY ASPARAGUS SOUP

## INGREDIENTS

2 pounds steamed asparagus, cooled

3 cups chicken broth

Salt and pepper, to taste

½ cup heavy cream

¼ cup crème fraiche, for garnish

## DIRECTIONS

1. Place all ingredients, except heavy cream and crème fraiche, into the 72-ounce Pitcher in the order listed.

2. PULSE 3 times and blend on 3 until smooth.

3. Add heavy cream and blend on 3 until combined.

4. Garnish each serving with crème fraiche and additional pepper.

DO NOT BLEND HOT INGREDIENTS.

**Prep time:** 15 minutes  **Cook time:** 35–40 minutes
**Container:** 72-ounce Pitcher
**Makes:** 6 servings

# BROCCOLI CHEDDAR SOUP

## INGREDIENTS

3 tablespoons butter

½ small yellow onion, chopped

1 medium carrot, peeled, chopped

2 tablespoons flour

3 cups chicken broth

3 cups broccoli florets

1 cup whole milk

¾ cup shredded cheddar cheese

Salt and pepper, to taste

## DIRECTIONS

1. Place butter into a heavy-bottom saucepan over medium heat; stir until melted. Add onion and carrot and cook until tender, about 5 minutes.

2. Whisk in the flour and cook 5 more minutes. Add broth and continue stirring as mixture thickens. Add broccoli and simmer over medium heat until tender, 20 to 25 minutes, stirring occasionally. Cool to room temperature.

3. Place cooled soup into the 72-ounce Pitcher. PULSE 3 times and blend on 3 until smooth.

4. Transfer the soup back to the saucepan. Add milk, cheese, salt, and pepper. Simmer until heated through.

DO NOT BLEND HOT INGREDIENTS.

**Prep time:** 15 minutes  **Cook time:** 40–45 minutes
**Container:** 72-ounce Pitcher
**Makes:** 8 servings

# BUTTERNUT SQUASH SOUP

## INGREDIENTS

3 tablespoons olive oil

1 large yellow onion, chopped

1 cup raw cashews

1 large apple, peeled, cored, chopped

1 large carrot, peeled, chopped

2 pounds butternut squash, cubed

1 teaspoon fresh thyme leaves

1 bay leaf

4 cups vegetable stock

Kosher salt and black pepper, to taste

## DIRECTIONS

1. Heat oil in a large saucepan over medium heat. Add the onion, cooking until it begins to soften, about 5 minutes. Add the cashews and cook, stirring, for about 5 minutes.

2. Add the apple, carrot, squash, thyme, and bay leaf to the saucepan and cook 5 minutes. Add the stock and stir to combine. Bring the soup to a boil and then reduce the heat to medium-low, allowing it to simmer until the squash is easily pierced with a knife, 20 to 25 minutes. Remove and discard bay leaf.

3. Allow the soup to cool to room temperature.

4. Working in two batches, ladle the cooled soup into the 72-ounce Pitcher. Blend on 2 until smooth.

5. Return soup to saucepan and simmer until heated through. Season with salt and pepper, to taste.

**DO NOT BLEND HOT INGREDIENTS.**

**Prep time:** 25 minutes  **Cook time:** 25 minutes
**Container:** 72-ounce Pitcher
**Makes:** 6 servings

# BLACK BEAN SOUP

## INGREDIENTS

1 teaspoon olive oil

½ onion, peeled, chopped

1 carrot, peeled, chopped

1 stalk celery, trimmed, chopped

2 cloves garlic, peeled, chopped

2 teaspoons cumin

1 teaspoon dried oregano

3 cups cooked black beans, drained

2 chipotle peppers

1 ¾ cups low-sodium chicken broth, plus more as desired

Salt and pepper, to taste

Sour cream, for garnish

Chives, for garnish

## DIRECTIONS

1. Heat oil in a 3-quart saucepan over medium-high heat. Add onion, carrot, celery, garlic, cumin, and oregano. Sauté until vegetables are softened. Cool to room temperature.

2. Place the cooled vegetables, black beans, chipotle peppers, chicken broth, salt, and pepper into the 72-ounce Pitcher.

3. PULSE 3 times and blend on 3 until smooth, about 60 seconds.

4. Return soup to saucepan and simmer until heated through.

5. Garnish each serving with sour cream and chives.

DO NOT BLEND HOT INGREDIENTS.

**Prep time:** 15 minutes  **Cook time:** 20 minutes
**Container:** 72-ounce Pitcher
**Makes:** 8 servings

# THAI CHICKEN COCONUT CURRY SOUP

## INGREDIENTS

2 tablespoons vegetable oil

3 cloves garlic, peeled

1 white onion, diced

3 cups coconut milk

3 cups chicken broth

3 tablespoons red curry paste

3 tablespoons soy sauce

3 tablespoons lime juice

1 tablespoon brown sugar

1 tablespoon ground turmeric

2 uncooked boneless chicken breasts, cut in 2-inch strips

4 cups rice stick noodles or vermicelli, cooked

1 cup bean sprouts, for garnish

Lime wedges, for garnish

Cilantro, chopped, for garnish

## DIRECTIONS

1. Heat oil in a stockpot. Add garlic and onion and sauté over medium heat until softened, about 10 minutes. Cool to room temperature.

2. Place the garlic and onion, coconut milk, chicken broth, curry paste, soy sauce, lime juice, brown sugar, and turmeric into the 72-ounce Pitcher.

3. Blend on 2 until smooth.

4. Return mixture to the stockpot, then add chicken and bring to a boil. Reduce heat and simmer for about 10 minutes, or until chicken is cooked through.

5. To serve, divide noodles between bowls. Ladle soup over noodles and garnish each serving with bean sprouts, a lime, and chopped cilantro.

**DO NOT BLEND HOT INGREDIENTS.**

**Prep time:** 10 minutes  **Cook time:** 10 minutes
**Container:** 72-ounce Pitcher
**Makes:** 3 servings

# PEP IN YOUR STEP SOUP

### INGREDIENTS

3 red bell peppers, roasted, peeled, cooled

¼ cup sundried tomatoes

2 cloves garlic, peeled

¼ cup white wine

¼ bunch Italian parsley, trimmed

1 cup low-sodium vegetable broth

Salt and pepper, to taste

Balsamic vinegar, for garnish

### DIRECTIONS

1. Place all ingredients, except balsamic vinegar, into the 72-ounce Pitcher in the order listed.

2. PULSE 3 times and blend on 3 until smooth.

3. Transfer soup to a medium saucepan and simmer until heated through, about 10 minutes. Serve warm in bowls garnished with a splash of balsamic vinegar, if desired.

**DO NOT BLEND HOT INGREDIENTS.**

**Prep time:** 20 minutes  **Cook time:** 1 hour
**Container:** 72-ounce Pitcher
**Makes:** 8 servings

# WHITE BEAN & CHICKEN CHILI

## INGREDIENTS

2 tablespoons olive oil

1 onion, chopped

1 green bell pepper, cored, chopped

3 cloves garlic, peeled, smashed

¾ pound uncooked boneless, skinless chicken breasts, chilled

Salt and pepper, to taste

1 tablespoon ground cumin

2 teaspoons dried oregano

1 teaspoon ground red chili pepper

3 cans (15 ounces each) cannellini beans (drain 2 cans)

2 cans (4 ounces each) diced green chiles

3 cups chicken broth

Shredded cheese, for garnish

Cilantro, chopped, for garnish

## DIRECTIONS

1. Place the oil into a large stockpot over medium heat. Add the onion, bell pepper, and garlic. Sauté and stir until softened.

2. Place the chicken into the 72-ounce Pitcher. PULSE 5 to 10 times, until finely ground.

3. Add the chicken to the stockpot along with the salt, pepper, cumin, oregano, and chili pepper. Stir in 2 cans drained beans, green chiles, and chicken broth.

4. Place remaining can of beans with liquid into the 72-ounce Pitcher. Blend on 2 until smooth. Add to chili and simmer 30 to 40 minutes, until slightly thickened.

5. Garnish each serving with shredded cheese and chopped cilantro.

**DO NOT BLEND HOT INGREDIENTS.**

**Prep time:** 20 minutes  **Cook time:** 40 minutes
**Container:** 72-ounce Pitcher
**Makes:** 4 servings

# PUMPKIN CURRY SOUP

## INGREDIENTS

1 teaspoon olive oil

1 white onion, chopped

½-inch piece fresh ginger, peeled, minced

1 tablespoon curry powder

1 can (15 ounces) pumpkin puree

1 ½ cups vegetable broth

1 ½ cups coconut milk, filtered, from a carton

2 teaspoons honey

½ teaspoon salt

Kale chips, for garnish

## DIRECTIONS

1. Place oil into a stockpot over medium-high heat. Add the onion, ginger, and curry powder. Sauté, stirring, until softened.

2. Add pumpkin puree, vegetable broth, coconut milk, honey, and salt. Simmer, stirring, about 15 minutes. Cool to room temperature.

3. Place soup into the 72-ounce Pitcher. Blend on 1 for 15 seconds. Blend on 2 until smooth, about 45 additional seconds.

4. Pour soup back into pot and simmer until heated through.

5. Serve in bowls, garnished with kale chips.

DO NOT BLEND HOT INGREDIENTS.

**Soak time:** 2 hours  **Prep time:** 15 minutes
**Container:** 72-ounce Pitcher
**Makes:** 6 servings

# CREAM OF BROCCOLI SOUP

## INGREDIENTS

1 cup raw cashews, soaked in water
for 2 hours, drained

4 cups vegetable broth, divided

6 cups broccoli, steamed, cooled

1 teaspoon garlic powder

Salt and pepper, to taste

## DIRECTIONS

1. Place all ingredients into the 72-ounce Pitcher in the order listed.

2. PULSE 3 times and blend on 3 until smooth.

3. Transfer soup to a saucepan. Simmer until heated through.

DO NOT BLEND HOT INGREDIENTS.

**Prep time:** 15 minutes  **Cook time:** 40 minutes
**Container:** 72-ounce Pitcher
**Makes:** 4 servings

# CAULIFLOWER WHITE CHEDDAR SOUP

## INGREDIENTS

4 cups cauliflower florets

½ small onion, peeled, cut in half

2 cups low-fat milk

¾ cup grated white cheddar cheese, plus additional for garnish

1 teaspoon onion powder

¾ teaspoon grated nutmeg, plus additional for garnish

Salt and pepper, to taste

## DIRECTIONS

1. Steam cauliflower with onion until tender, about 15 minutes. Cool to room temperature.

2. Place cooled cauliflower and onion into the 72-ounce Pitcher. PULSE 3 times and blend on 3 until smooth.

3. Transfer pureed cauliflower and onion to a stockpot, add remaining ingredients, and simmer until heated through.

4. Garnish each serving with grated cheese and nutmeg.

**DO NOT BLEND HOT INGREDIENTS.**

**Prep time:** 10 minutes  **Cook time:** 20 minutes
**Container:** 72-ounce Pitcher
**Makes:** 4 cups

# SPINACH ARTICHOKE DIP

## INGREDIENTS

¼ cup mayonnaise

¼ cup sour cream

1 package (8 ounces) cream cheese

2 tablespoons lemon juice

½ cup low-fat shredded mozzarella cheese

¼ cup grated Parmesan cheese

4 cloves garlic, peeled

1 can (14 ounces) artichoke hearts, drained

1 cup frozen spinach, thawed, squeezed of excess liquid

Sliced French bread or pita chips, for serving

## DIRECTIONS

1. Preheat oven to 350°F.

2. Place mayonnaise, sour cream, cream cheese, lemon juice, mozzarella cheese, Parmesan cheese, and garlic into the 72-ounce Pitcher.

3. Blend on 2 until ingredients are thoroughly combined, about 30 seconds.

4. Add artichokes and spinach, then PULSE 5 times, until evenly incorporated.

5. Spoon dip into a heat-resistant serving dish and bake 20 minutes. Serve warm with sliced French bread or pita chips.

**DO NOT BLEND HOT INGREDIENTS.**

**Prep time:** 10 minutes  **Cook time:** 25 minutes
**Container:** 72-ounce Pitcher
**Makes:** 2–4 servings

# SUN-DRIED TOMATO SAUCE

## INGREDIENTS

1 onion, cut in quarters

4 cloves garlic, peeled

1 tablespoon canola oil

1 can (28 ounces) whole tomatoes and juice

1 jar (6 ounces) sun-dried tomatoes packed in olive oil

½ cup dry red wine

½ teaspoon red pepper flakes

Salt and pepper, to taste

¼ bunch basil, chopped

## DIRECTIONS

1. Place the onion and the garlic into the 72-ounce Pitcher. PULSE until roughly chopped.

2. Heat the oil in a medium saucepan over medium heat. Add the onions and garlic. Sauté for 5 minutes, or until softened.

3. Place the tomatoes with juice, sun-dried tomatoes, red wine, and red pepper flakes into the 72-ounce Pitcher. Blend on 1 for 15 seconds, or until a chunky consistency is achieved.

4. Add the tomato sauce to the saucepan with garlic and onion. Add salt and pepper to taste. Simmer for 20 minutes.

5. Garnish with fresh basil before serving.

**DO NOT BLEND HOT INGREDIENTS.**

# SWEET HOT BARBECUE SAUCE

## INGREDIENTS

1 cup ketchup

¼ cup dark brown sugar, packed

¼ cup Worcestershire sauce

3 tablespoons apple cider vinegar

1 teaspoon hot sauce

2 teaspoons garlic powder

2 teaspoons onion powder

½ teaspoon dry mustard powder

1 teaspoon celery seed

2 tablespoons lemon juice

1 tablespoon lemon zest

## DIRECTIONS

1. Place all ingredients into the 72-ounce Pitcher in the order listed.

2. Blend on 2 until very smooth.

3. Transfer sauce to a small saucepan over medium heat. Bring just to a boil, then reduce heat and simmer for 5 minutes.

4. When mixture is cooled, pour into a clear jar with a tightly sealed lid. Refrigerate up to 2 weeks.

**DO NOT BLEND HOT INGREDIENTS.**

**Prep time:** 5 minutes  **Cook time:** 1 hour
**Container:** 72-ounce Pitcher
**Makes:** 4 cups

# CHIPOTLE SALSA

## INGREDIENTS

2 cans (10 ounces each) whole peeled tomatoes

1 small white onion, cut in quarters

1 jalapeño pepper, cut in half, seeds removed

1 canned chipotle pepper, in adobo sauce

2 tablespoons adobo sauce

1 bunch cilantro, stems removed

1 lime, peeled, cut in quarters, seeds removed

Salt and pepper, to taste

## DIRECTIONS

1. Place all ingredients into the 72-ounce Pitcher in the order listed.

2. PULSE until desired consistency is achieved.

3. Cover and refrigerate at least 1 hour before serving.

# FIRE-ROASTED TOMATO SALSA

## INGREDIENTS

2 cans (10 ounces each) tomatoes

1 white onion, cut in quarters

1 jalapeño pepper, seeds removed

1 canned chipotle chile pepper, with
2 tablespoons adobo sauce

1 bunch cilantro, stems trimmed

1 lime, peeled, cut in quarters, seeds removed

Salt and pepper, to taste

## DIRECTIONS

1. Place all ingredients into the 72-ounce Pitcher in the order listed.

2. PULSE until desired consistency is achieved.

3. Cover and refrigerate at least 1 hour before serving.

**Prep time:** 10 minutes
**Container:** 72-ounce Pitcher
**Makes:** 6–8 servings

# PINEAPPLE CILANTRO DIPPING SAUCE

## INGREDIENTS

3 cups pineapple chunks

1 ½ small serrano chiles, seeds removed

1 small white onion, cut in quarters

½ cup cilantro

¼ cup lime juice

3 tablespoons coconut oil

Salt and pepper, to taste

## DIRECTIONS

**1.** Place all ingredients into the 72-ounce Pitcher in the order listed.

**2.** PULSE until desired consistency is achieved.

**Prep time:** 5 minutes
**Container:** 72-ounce Pitcher
**Makes:** 4 servings

# JAMAICAN SCREWDRIVER

## INGREDIENTS

½ cup vodka

¼ cup light rum

2 cups orange juice

1 cup frozen pineapple chunks

2 cups ice

4 orange slices, for garnish

## DIRECTIONS

1. Place all ingredients, except orange slices, into the 72-ounce Pitcher in the order listed.

2. PULSE 3 times and blend on 3 until smooth.

3. Pour into chilled glasses and garnish with orange slices.

**Prep time:** 5 minutes
**Container:** 72-ounce Pitcher
**Makes:** 3 servings

# FROZEN JOE

## INGREDIENTS

1 cup strong black coffee, chilled

1 cup low-fat dark chocolate frozen yogurt

2 tablespoons chocolate sauce

2 tablespoons caramel sauce

½ cup dark rum

10 ice cubes

2 tablespoons whipped cream, for garnish

## DIRECTIONS

1. Place all ingredients, except whipped cream, into the 72-ounce Pitcher in the order listed.

2. Blend on 3 until smooth.

3. Serve in tall glasses garnished with whipped cream.

**DO NOT BLEND HOT INGREDIENTS.**

**Prep time:** 10 minutes
**Container:** 72-ounce Pitcher
**Makes:** 6 servings

# WATERMELON BASIL SANGRIA

## INGREDIENTS

3 cups watermelon chunks

¼ cup fresh basil, stems removed

2 limes, peeled, cut in half, seeds removed

½ cup brandy

1 cup dry white wine

3 tablespoons agave nectar

1 cup frozen peaches

2 ¼ cups ice

## DIRECTIONS

1. Place all ingredients into the 72-ounce Pitcher in the order listed.

2. PULSE 3 times and blend on 3 until smooth.

**Prep time:** 10 minutes
**Container:** 72-ounce Pitcher
**Makes:** 4 servings

# PEAR GINGER SAKE MARTINI

## INGREDIENTS

1 frozen pear, peeled, cored

½ teaspoon grated fresh ginger

2 cups pear juice

½ to ¾ cup sake

1 tablespoon agave nectar

1 cup ice

4 crystallized ginger pieces, slit partway through, for garnish

## DIRECTIONS

1. Place all ingredients, except crystallized ginger, into the 72-ounce Pitcher in the order listed.

2. PULSE 3 times and blend on 3 until smooth.

3. Pour into chilled martini glasses and garnish each with a piece of crystallized ginger.

**Prep time:** 10 minutes
**Container:** 72-ounce Pitcher
**Makes:** 8 servings

# TROPICAL COOLER

## INGREDIENTS

1 cup pineapple chunks

½ jalapeño pepper, seeds removed

½-inch piece fresh ginger, peeled

⅓ English cucumber, peeled, cut in quarters

Juice of 1 ½ limes

1 ½ cups coconut water

½ cup silver tequila

3 tablespoons agave nectar

¼ teaspoon ground coriander

3 ½ cups frozen mango chunks

1 ½ cups ice

Cucumber slices, for garnish

## DIRECTIONS

1. Place all ingredients, except cucumber slices, into the 72-ounce Pitcher in the order listed.

2. PULSE 3 times and blend on 3 until smooth.

3. Pour into glasses and garnish each with a slice of cucumber.

**Prep time:** 5 minutes
**Container:** 72-ounce Pitcher
**Makes:** 3 servings

# FROZEN MARGARITA

## INGREDIENTS

¾ cup tequila

¼ cup triple sec

¼ cup lime juice

⅓ cup water

¾ cup frozen limeade

2 cups ice

## DIRECTIONS

1. Place all ingredients into the 72-ounce Pitcher in the order listed.

2. PULSE 3 times and blend on 3 until smooth, about 45 seconds.

# BLUEBERRY HONEY CUCUMBER MOJITO

## INGREDIENTS

1 cup English cucumber, chopped

2 ½ cups blueberries

4 mint leaves

¾ cup pear juice

1 cup light rum

2 tablespoons honey

3 cups ice

## DIRECTIONS

1.  Place all ingredients into the 72-ounce Pitcher in the order listed.

2.  PULSE 3 times and blend on 3 until smooth.

**Prep time:** 5 minutes
**Container:** 72-ounce Pitcher
**Makes:** 6 servings

# LEM-MOSA

## INGREDIENTS

3 lemons, peeled, cut in half, seeds removed

4 mint leaves

1 ¾ cups dry white wine

2 tablespoons agave nectar

3 ½ cups ice

## DIRECTIONS

1. Place all ingredients into the 72-ounce Pitcher in the order listed.

2. PULSE 3 times and blend on 3 until smooth, about 60 seconds.

**Prep time:** 10 minutes
**Container:** 72-ounce Pitcher
**Makes:** 5 servings

# STRAWBERRY DAIQUIRI

## INGREDIENTS

4 cups strawberries, hulled, cut in half

1 cup lime juice

1 cup light rum

2 cups ice

## DIRECTIONS

1. Place all ingredients into the 72-ounce Pitcher in the order listed.

2. PULSE 3 times and blend on 3 until smooth.

**Prep time:** 5 minutes
**Container:** 72-ounce Pitcher
**Makes:** 4 servings

# FROZEN WHITE SIBERIAN

## INGREDIENTS

½ cup coffee-flavored liqueur, plus additional for garnish

⅓ cup vodka

½ cup low-fat milk

1 cup nonfat coffee-flavored frozen yogurt or ice cream

1 cup ice

Whipped cream, for garnish

## DIRECTIONS

1. Place all ingredients, except whipped cream, into the 72-ounce Pitcher in the order listed.

2. PULSE 3 times and blend on 3 until smooth.

3. Top with whipped cream.

**Prep time:** 5 minutes
**Container:** 72-ounce Pitcher
**Makes:** 6 servings

# BANANA COLADA

## INGREDIENTS

1 cup light rum

2 cups pineapple juice

1 cup light coconut milk

2 small frozen ripe bananas, cut in half

2 cups frozen pineapple chunks

1 cup ice

## DIRECTIONS

1. Place all ingredients into the 72-ounce Pitcher in the order listed.

2. PULSE 3 times and blend on 3 until smooth.

**Prep time:** 5 minutes
**Container:** 72-ounce Pitcher
**Makes:** 4 servings

# CHOCOLATE ALMOND DELIGHT

## INGREDIENTS

1 cup chocolate frozen yogurt

1 cup vanilla frozen yogurt

3 tablespoons coconut milk

⅓ cup amaretto liqueur

¼ cup dark crème de cacao

½ cup almond milk

½ cup ice

## DIRECTIONS

1. Place all ingredients into the 72-ounce Pitcher in the order listed.

2. PULSE 3 times and blend on 3 until smooth.

**Prep time:** 15 minutes
**Container:** 72-ounce Pitcher
**Makes:** 4 servings

# CANTALOUPE PEPPER FREEZE

## INGREDIENTS

2 cups frozen cantaloupe chunks

½ teaspoon freshly ground black pepper

¾ cups water, plus more if needed

1 cup ice

## DIRECTIONS

1. Place all ingredients into the 72-ounce Pitcher in the order listed.

2. PULSE 3 times and blend on 2 until smooth. Add additional water if needed.

**Prep time:** 15 minutes  **Chill time:** 2 hours
**Container:** 72-ounce Pitcher
**Makes:** 4 servings

# BANANA CHOCOLATE MOUSSE

## INGREDIENTS

2 ripe bananas, cut in quarters

2 ripe avocados, peeled, cut in quarters, pits removed

¼ cup chocolate syrup

Juice of ½ orange

¼ cup cocoa powder

## DIRECTIONS

**1.** Place all ingredients into the 72-ounce Pitcher in the order listed.

**2.** Blend on 2 until smooth, scraping down sides of Pitcher as needed.

**3.** Place mousse into an airtight container and refrigerate until chilled, about 2 hours.

**Prep time:** 5 minutes
**Container:** 72-ounce Pitcher
**Makes:** 4 servings

# VANILLA NUT FROZEN TREAT

## INGREDIENTS

1 cup vanilla oat milk

½ cup walnut halves

1 cup nonfat vanilla yogurt

½ teaspoon pure vanilla extract

2 packets (.035 ounce each) stevia

2 ½ cups ice

## DIRECTIONS

1. Place all ingredients into the 72-ounce Pitcher in the order listed.

2. PULSE 3 times and blend on 3 until smooth, about 45 seconds.

**Prep time:** 10 minutes
**Container:** 72-ounce Pitcher
**Makes:** 4 servings

# FROZEN STRAWBERRY PEACH TREAT

## INGREDIENTS

½ cup whole milk

¼ cup low-fat vanilla yogurt

2 tablespoons agave nectar

1 teaspoon vanilla extract

1 ½ cups frozen strawberries

½ cup frozen peaches

## DIRECTIONS

1. Place all ingredients into the 72-ounce Pitcher in the order listed.

2. Blend on 3 until smooth and creamy.

3. Garnish with your favorite fruit toppings.

**Prep time:** 10 minutes **Freeze time:** 3–4 hours
**Container:** 72-ounce Pitcher
**Makes:** 2–4 servings

# WATERMELON MINT GRANITA

## INGREDIENTS

6 cups watermelon chunks

1 tablespoon lime juice

3 tablespoons agave nectar

6 mint leaves

## DIRECTIONS

1. Place all ingredients into the 72-ounce Pitcher in the order listed.

2. Blend on 3 until smooth. Strain mixture and discard pulp.

3. Pour mixture into ice cube trays. Freeze 3 to 4 hours, or until almost solid.

4. To serve, shave with a fork into small glasses.

**Prep time:** 5 minutes
**Container:** 72-ounce Pitcher
**Makes:** 4 servings

# COCONUT PINEAPPLE SORBET

## INGREDIENTS

½ cup light coconut milk

1 tablespoon fresh lime juice

1 tablespoon agave nectar

1 teaspoon grated fresh ginger

1 small frozen ripe banana

1 cup frozen pineapple chunks

## DIRECTIONS

1. Place all ingredients into the 72-ounce Pitcher in the order listed.

2. Blend on 3 until smooth and creamy.

# Index

Questions? 1-877-646-5288

| | |
|---|---|
| Lem-Mosa | 47 |
| Pear Ginger Sake Martini | 43 |
| Strawberry Daiquiri | 48 |
| Tropical Cooler | 44 |
| Watermelon Basil Sangria | 42 |

## DESSERTS

| | |
|---|---|
| Banana Chocolate Mousse | 53 |
| Cantaloupe Pepper Freeze | 52 |
| Coconut Pineapple Sorbet | 57 |
| Frozen Strawberry Peach Treat | 55 |
| Vanilla Nut Frozen Treat | 54 |
| Watermelon Mint Granita | 56 |

# Notes

# Notes